Tongo Eisen-Martin crosses boundaries and borders, gives voice to those who need to be heard, and gives us a language for the pain and beauty of an ongoing struggle for a better, more just tomorrow.

Farah Jasmine Griffin

Eyes and ears are just innocent bystanders as his semiautomatic ink does a drive by on the unconscious. Harriet would have freed a thousand more of us if she had a shotgun in one hand and this brother's book in the other. Don't believe the hype? Read on."

Bryonn Bain

Unflinching in its gaze, someone's dead already is concerned with the meticulous painting of human beings struggling everyday not to be food for the machine and the aftermath and pile of broken lives lying in the wake. The beauty of these poems is the imagery. The power of these poems is how the imagery removes the makeup and pulls back the bandage, forcing us to see the scars and sores of our lives.

C. Leigh McInnis

There is a particular skill in phrasing the rhythms of one's own generation and the metaphors of these times in a way that embraces culture and transcends race, acknowledges family and uplifts community, is African-American in sensibility and world citizen at its heart. Eisen-Martin is an estimable wordsmith whose poems are full of courage and music and someone's dead already is an excellent volume.

devorah major

someone's dead already spits life fire into the soul's of everyone within living and breathing distance. Eisen-Martin speaks in the tongue of liberation and the language of action. Baraka, Tupac, Maya, Sekou Sundiaita and all the ancestor word-warriors — be at peace — the torch has been passed and burns brightly in the griot soldier hands of a poet named Tongo Eisen-Martin

Jamal Joseph

someone's dead already

Tongo Eisen-Martin

Much
Love
Always

Bootstrap Press
2015

First Edition, 5th Printing

ISBN 13: 978-0-9886108-3-5

Typesetting & Book Design by Derek Fenner.
Cover Art by Biko Eisen-Martin.

Bootstrap Press books are designed and edited by Derek Fenner and Ryan Gallagher.

West Coast:
365 Euclid Ave, # 107
Oakland, CA 94610

East Coast:
31 Wyman Street
Lowell, MA 01852

www.bootstrapproductions.org

The dedication:

We had the funeral in the garage
But I think he was long gone

A narrator on distant rooftops
Smoking with new friends

Repeating

From a two floor skyline
An abandoned house talked to me
It said young man
>> You are heroic
>> And ten years old

Among twenty generations of friends. Friends will free fall away.
Free fall up.
Free fall to walls with fifth grade speed to industrial paint behind
second-hand fences

Young man, use quick knife tones. Be bone and brass. Be last laugh
music.

You are always leaving. Always one change of clothes from the door.
A life in escape.

Two floor skyline said you are the guide that dies in the middle

>> The friend more blues than skin

>> The face that cheap hotel schizophrenics can place
>> With 90 miles per hour right eyes

Among dry heat killers
Once children
Three feet high
And roaming
And repeating
And aiming
At cotton mirrors that hang on breathing walls

You are ten years old   Tagging along
          Yawning at well-lit violence

Whistling tool shop songs
You will be useful

You will be high and alone
Flying on a nephew dragon
From a twenty dollar family
In a sky that calls itself
Just more soil

                                        Around walls
                                        That are just walls
                                        Except these walls
                                        Suggest you make wives
                                        Out of highs and currency

          Here the air is polite to sleepy glass and bullying walls.

Young man,
You will admit
That sometimes
Suicide is power
                    Some people live stronger as ghosts

And sometimes the afterlife empties
    Billions of souls
              Enter objects
                    Like playground bullets
And abandoned door frames. Even broken glass will prove it has
voice too.

There are 24 hours behind your back
                              Look over your shoulder right now
                              Can you hear it?

The sound of drums punching themselves out. The sound of piano parts learned in between assassination attempts.

Be bone and brass. Be bone enough for two souls. Be invincible again

Suffer
Red-eyed accents. Professional fingertips. Our gifted victims. Six in the morning beer. The first month of probation.
        —The shout at the wall

See these words that shouldn't be home

> Look behind you again
> Be invincible again
> Be Windward
> Be a sad machete
> Be her son
> Be a thief
> Steal them back
> Laugh too long
> Never look away

The afterlife will empty

        And walk you home

Venezuela. Live from the 10th floor. A poem

The Bronx got a balcony
                         for Martin Luther King
Somewhere in Caracas

Only this time
Martin claps the president
                It starts with graffiti
On the highway
              That mostly says:
Freedom fighters ain't dying alone this year
And   the Bronx   Ain't dying   this century

And Barlovento decided
                         Compromise Is Not A Strategy

And
God tells the truth on every floor / And under every roof

In ten canyons of rising slums
I mean
Colony Rising
I mean
stacks and stacks of window bars / Wash the mountain sides
With Bay Area war stories
Colonies
Back rising

Baby heroes and hero babies
got   mural'd   concrete

              For   blankets
                Martin got a machete

                    And   the   Bronx
              Shares   shoes   and   skylines
                    With   Caracas

And   there's   only   one   casket   /   For   all   of   us

I mean
Your living room / I have earned
And my great grandmother: Is here too
And she soldiers every night
                    By hero babies
                              and other things rising

I collect what she has earned
And:
"Here, no one surrenders"
I mean.
Be home

Soon

Commercial Break

Settler culture stands a chance in theaters
      Along with ivy league students
            And drug dealers who have gone drug dealer

                    The superintendent
                    Is in the details
                    In a century
                    Where people get
                    multiple choice therapy
                    And designer eviction notices
                    Cuff yourself breakfast programs
                    Kill three people
                    Get your next happy meal free
                    Get your next job for cheap

          Preteen go back to Africa
             AFRICA GO BACK TO AFRICA

Rat on your father's ashes and change your first name
Rub ointment on your test scores
Return your borrowed cable
They selling year long lasting naps

Did you hear about the first black rapper in 50 years?
He was executed by the mayor

Cars for curtains
         The mayor lives in peace
         And watches bummed cigarettes
             Dance to the late 90s moods
             Of people who are
The first

Second
And last to die

> A sellout is born every California minute
> In a case manager's heaven

Rushed shrugs in waves of bystanders

Apparently
God does not save kings   And pigs save time

Rushed shrugs
By satellite raised cowards
Northern dope to northern democrats

Weekdays like this

> White supremacists love uniforms
> And other exercises in brainless self-talk

I will always fail to see the modernity here

> White supremacists who are white
> See with cross hair glee
> All the whacks they can take during commercial breaks

10 feet to commercial break—two miles of commercial break—
commercial breaks between commercial breaks—treaty ink all over a
gutted neighborhood—the commercial break

white supremacists who are white   snort holiday massacres

> my friend rolled 40 blunts on a bible
> another beat himself to death

my mother cried during holiday massacres
another has worked them all
my uncle's mug shot taught me nothing
and my aunt never tells us to be safe when leaving her house
instead she reminds us
it's a good day to die

Pollution

He watches cable
    While the TV watches suicide
        A watery coma talks to the last thought of his life
            Says
            Don't you know it is all second hand smoke
            Says
            Put your trust in me and I will make sure you are spoken
            Says
            Take me to your leader, sucka
            Says
            Aw man I'm just fuckin with ya
            Says
            Yeah, I'm gonna miss him too

        Coma ignores air
The air dresses in haze and chemical fits of softening red
        Coma ignores sun
The sun is in the living room
        Unbothered by the pollution
            The city is also in the living room
                Unbothered by love stories
                    Childhood still visits this living room
                       Outside

Childhood visits in threes
A flash calls the air to come home   In chemical fits of
hardening red   *Make sure you're spoken   When the street
goes weightless   And cousins in vertigo   Make windows fire*
        Chemical fits of homelessness   Chemical fits of
genocide   half the city is   walking home
In threes   In second hand smoke   And repast
conversations   Sick world love story   In a beggars balance
        Who watches last walks   Watches a little bit of this city

The short end of a contracting red life   *Miss him too*
          He might be loved   just not in this living room
          Same air Same red Same city   *Different love story*
all   Second   hand   *s m o k e*

hear the bullet news   hear the bullet neighbors   the November
of the gun line
a future spoken in walls   while he paints a four wall mural   with
cigarette burns
cheekbones for brushes   throwing dice through the wall
          coma ignores gun shots

don't you know it is all second hand smoke / don't you know half the city is
walking home / in threes / in love   a street in the woods   axe in
the air   under the heads of   old
brotherhoods   not a sight for first kisses just old cars and
new house paint

          do not get too drunk / ghosts hate to see you this way / in
this living room
with the last thought of his life / I might be loved

          Just:

          not here

Blood In My Eye

Guided by teeth
Goes the country
      There's a cow's mouth on the flag

Peculiar notepad holds street life dear
But the writer aint here
He's somewhere talking to tombstones about the good ol' days—Or
splashing reborn water on his latest face
      Or wondering how his old gun is doing in the afterlife
Wondering how much death trap is in those gas station aisles.
There's got to be a million dollars a day on this concrete island. New
engine in the moon. Why it never goes down. I mean 72 straight
hours of night…At least according to everyone's posture around
here.

8:30 in the morning is really 30 minutes to closing

                                              The city

shuts down for a sleepy rat race
Elevators   shoe shuffle   to the nearest   heaven
Laughing with rats the whole ways up. There are scabs every damn
where. In puddles of city. In concentrated schools. In tv lit warm
rooms. The light reveals military fatigue when it hits just right
on the ties that are wrapped around the necks of lazy white guys.
EMPIRE IS TOO EASY BABY. CHANT AT THE WALLS ALL
SUMMER IF YOU FEEL LIKE IT.

Best way for a target to move is shooting back.
Running for a tree line made of freeways
Wisdom says, against a war machine on Tuesdays, you stand no
chance.
BUT MAY WE BE THE LAST POOR MEN TO PLAY IT SAFE

Cow's mouth on the flag
Politician raises his hand
And the crowd shows their teeth

Oligarch raises his hand
And little girls are not safe outside

You are all high, depressed, and comrades in function. Fifteen
minutes to closing and the city has survived another Black
rebellion. Stay down, my love. We just paying dues by trash fires
not just anyone can set. Don't you love how deadly things whisper
in the moment and men kill like
feathers fall
while everyone is screaming inside
The writer knows that death is not a matter of dignity. Rather humor.
In a house that smells like roach races. Nuclear percentages on torn
stoves.
I mean here: life never was   just lazy matches and manic
inhumanity   hands rushing away from life   towards stoves

What are we doing here?
Surviving, baby
For no reason in particular
See, nobody's gone far today
Nobody will go far tomorrow
Trust me,
Hell
And Heaven
Cannot count

Strange gardens
Where second hand clothes play
And concrete wishes to be human
Only to be cannibal
Where they find you drenched

                          And drains wish to be human
                  Only to be worthy arms for you to die in

GREET THEM ALL, GRANDSON. PREPARE FOR THE
DAY WHEN EVERY CHILD IS CALM. AND DON'T SAY
WE GHOSTS DIDN'T WRITE YOU A POEM.
Don't say
            we didn't dig your life.
Remember the shotgun by the coat rack that everybody in
the house knows how to use. Remember the tightrope made of needles
for walking in between driveways. And man-made best friends. Go
ahead, Grandson. Tune the street again. *Never mind this country kills
musicians first.*

Broken neck nights
Scarred neck life
If these walls could write lyrics
            What's your angle, angel eyes?
Thirty to fifty rounds pass by
On a street with no daughters this street has no sons   *just*
young prisoners of war
In a racist city that means to make capital

                                    And we know so much
                                          We know it all
                              We were stood against walls

Who's on the third cross around here?
Cow's moth salivating over the street

            —And that is the story of why we aim at teeth.

A Short Movie

This is the poem I've been avoiding for two hours
The one where the hero dies in jail
And she forgets him in three damn months
That's all he had to work with apparently
But why did he have to die in jail?

Day One. The First Part

Enough of the noise makes it to the conversation I will have
tomorrow night with the woman I love.

I will tell her about a world I once saw end.

The Universe will have nothing on her decision.

Associative

I was better with a pint in the car at settling down. And you didn't mind. "better he spend money on liquor than gas." I almost wrote a song for a porch yesterday. But then I remembered what happened last time. It was the beginning of the end. And besides, I don't compliment dresses often. Must mean we are married. Which means the first line wasn't necessary. Or more necessary than ever. You have misunderstood skin. It is a two-way stage in a world of no crowds. I need to write this outside. Where none of my family lives and I don't know every angle of the altar. Outside, where I don't know what your hall lights will say next. Where your number don't work. Where I got more serious looking friends. I mean I was just thinking about you and your cigarette. Baby, I had it bad. Worse than you, if you can believe that. I remember every night trying to care for two weeks straight. From midnight to two in the morning. And just like now, I took a lot of breaks and ignored the rules, like by now I should have set the ransom money on fire. Pistol by this porch, baby. This porch aint for you. This is my blue phase, baby. Blue phase. Then body drop. Then my blank luck. Then my phone rings. Then she's a window at four in the morning. Then I believe in nothing. Then I forget to eat. Then I know what line is next. Then you do too. But let me say that the night air got nothing on my name. They say lions destroy all but that last home. When hotel doors come true and spirits don't take sides, the loving is good and sort of all over the place. Let's not say anything for the next five minutes and also the last ten minutes tomorrow. Has the liquor run its course? Woke up a new intellectual with a girlfriend and no bad habits. I can unmake that porch if you want. Go ahead and take all the 1:37 AM you need. Has gravity ever wished to defy you? Can you take my heart rate home while I crash at my lady's house? She won't let it sleep on the couch. I told her it'd be well-behaved. But no. It reminds her of runaway buses. Love/hate relationship, I'd say.

Project Fence and Central Time

Gated puppet dances alone
Bars and jig
Says
I am the happy one of legion

                              Meanwhile
                        Kids commit childhood
                      Behind wood and plaster joints

                                                              Wire dodgers
                                              Under this silly puppet
                              A silly puppet dancing for white heaven
                                                          The puppet is

A Story that the United States is Made of

A white child can
Send any number
To hell
Whether one demon
Or a whole horde
Something white
Will win
In the end

So get as close
To whiteness
As possible
Where it's safe
And there's honey
And Monday isn't so bad
And God will give you a pass
If you respect the flag
And watch enough television
Ignore a lot of yourself
Ignore a lot of us
Or flip the switch
Push the button
On behalf of white children

Or pass me a funky soda
Stocked in 1998
Or a beer
From the devil's bartender
Gas station and saloon

I never threw rocks
At the crazy lady

Just bricks at myself
Like the gas station
Got a basement
And I'm at home
Under 1998

And
some white child somewhere
Wants to be my best friend
So I better
Prepare for the day we meet

The Chamber of Willie B.

Bed Stuy rooftop is more stage than watchtower

I remember the play / I prepare to land / Loved one is there / We will never be here again / Our lives in reunion / Lightening for shade To keep us blue   She sips sangria / The devil drinks cranberry juice / And looks all the time / At the watch his mother bought / The devil gets a birthday too / And a summer / And her short story / She sips   slow

Slight of lightening. Our little brother is the sky. Now we don't panic.   Whatever's gone is not lost

This brotherhood needs a cardboard box / This street needs better roti / Not another Giuliani-ite / This brotherhood uses lightning for shade / This street needs one more character / Who wanders This rooftop is a three king theater
On the warm black coast of July   We will never be here again

For Lejauhn.

His little brother taught me / That Monday gathers its steel, bedrock / and billy clubs / Gathers its pixel empires, gun industries, and blood stretched shoe cloth / Gathers its last breaths, reddening eyes, and hours old vigils / Then drops itself on hand shakes / Taught me / To always holler at the window

Won't be working class by tomorrow

1.
Capitalists dropped ten tons of barbed wire on my Tuesday shift
We shot back at the chimpanzee pilots for the sport

The contractor has already smoked three cigars, only an hour into
my court appearance shift
my supervisor says he likes the smell. reminds him of when he ran
the streets
and all I remember is we shot back

2.
        I am breaking fingers for my sister's bill collectors
Garage
casket
open
All third world parallels kill openly
Breaking my lungs for my sister's rent
Slave quarters glass craftsman
Sculptor of construction dust
I miss Hennessey by midmorning
I miss cigarettes by sun down
I miss murder by inches

                                    Five dollar bills cherish
                                        My days outside
                                        Always behind

3.
Reoccurring cliff
Two blocks up
Along with slavers' paraphernalia
                    Along with an ordinary pan handler
Along with ethnic parade history

Along with ethnic parade
Along with 13th graders
But let's talk about the fact
That four dead children later
I still don't have a problem with beating you up in front of everybody
Let's talk about the fact that money is death

Down to my last five bucks
—a shoe

10 O'clock political education
—a dream

I got the job
—a blues

two days later
—a cliff

4.

title intersection / a city's beginning and end / everything
talks / except people / masses, baby, masses / industry and heaven
above us / on our faces / like backs / backs like oblivion / look down
here / we will listen to the war stories you cough / we dig war
stories / and December health / we dig masses / hell aint so
bad / where nobody commits treason / or hides face from
neighbors / there's not one cousin down here / so dig the class
loyalty / street fires and world war steam sound cozy / beer label
blankets / and some drugs done somewhere around here / bottle for
bottle / goes left foot and right foot / story for story they
go / December for December / Not one mention of cousins / Just
industry and heaven / Dig the masses / Dig the toothy
oblivion / Where shoulders begin / Where cities end / Where backs
are faces / The title of our dream

Waiting for Prints

Like weapon is to jacket and precinct holds Friday hostage. Fossil
Jaw then Judge

Tunnel at the end of the light
See an overtime hurricane smacking more houses

> sleep
> until
> woke by
> dry
> cereal
> and
> surrend
> --er

This holding cell only needs a giant pan handler's palms
To shake these coin men around

Pass

The smoke was infant like me

Nothing was careful on that corner
Especially not these young twins
And we were twins
Not in mother
But in mothering
Not in father
But in foundation
Adjusting to the ramble of 90's check cashing lines
And birthday beers
Adjusting to the city alphabet
Learning the first names
Of liquor store owners
And their nephews
And we would meet in the middle of all this
Who was the genius
Who was the distraction
Depends on the teeth of the narrator
I cut mine that day
Although I didn't know it
Rambles of 90's war
Capital was always coming
But in the mean time
I was gonna dive in
And not even pretend that
I knew what I was doing

Things You Never Said

My name will be the last one to see me alive / The only one to see me again / My name is borrowed with sand / Borrowed by sand / A month of last times / I am from an interstate fortune told / I live like a shot glass isn't scared to drop

365

Heroin in my smile
Mountain made of flatland robbery
Among some things on my mind
The last store run in the name of shared afterlife
Friday to the filter
Tall tale on earth
Looking down when I walk
Here's to that angel
That never appeared to america
And a night of dog paddle
And a batch of hangovers looking for a home

Climbing Back Down the Wind

There were hammers in my cradle.
Which made some people scared to check on me.

Because God would have a devil
And State street would have a resurrection
And I would be a menace. Menace to veins. Veins that the city
     protects with precinct flesh.

                    You know people actually work and marry here!?
                    The Sun actually comes up!?

Have you heard the one about ghetto dwellers?
Bang. They all duck.

Well look what the heathen drug in. What is that my bullet? Who is
that your son? Have you heard the one about last names?

Did you know that late night talk is the car door to the soul—*I*
don't think we've been here before. In some type of criminal heaven.
Controlling every headlight for miles.

                    If the journey has pain
                    It's the way I came

My name is on this sea! Royalty among mimes would be my right
hand. Or it would be a brand new hammer. Or wolf traveling at the
speed cities end. Interpretations of shot men.

You know hands are the only place souls are actually found. And fists get
a road trip too.

                    Maybe you should mind me

                              Or maybe I paid too much attention to this black coat
                                    As I was growing up in this wrong lit room
                                          At least the walls were nice guys

At least I had this sea.
At least I got this ocean
when her words freeze and Central Time is up
when my family relapses into suicidal neighborhoods and can't
    depend on me
when Black children are sad
when there are guns everywhere
when death is here and I'm a new kind of near-sighted. And she's a new
    kind of lovely; death is.

                                          Rites of front yard passage
                                             Getting people beat up
                                          I say: I'm not paranoid enough
                                          You got a taste for violence!?

        I've winked at three funerals. The Lord gave his only begotten…
                                                 temper…to me
                                          Death knows me by nickname
                                             I call her nothing cute

                                    Lord, let me see the enemy in my circle
                                    Let me see that the enemy is my circle
                                             Let my circle kill me
                                             Let me not stay dead

I will wink again

I remember who I am down to the street signs. Streets pass my life
back and forth. Pass me under gambler jokes and cigarettes; and here
I am thinking that this is what you call driving at night. Or this is
what you call thirty five miles away. Freeway and awe smeared all
over the city. Tell me. How do you write letters with a building on

top of your head? With a building feasting on you? With a thousand backs turned to your kids? *Without her subtle gesture to interpret?* In the middle of a backfired resurrection with a president who is out to kill you?

We only got one
gun to speak of
Still we sleep
good in august
And nobody
talks back in
traffic
Interestingly
handsome
bastard
Hat to match a
violent song
High hat on its
own
Motherless
though less of a
child
Project tiles
become tires
Choirs suck
down liquor
Five floors
become
audience for a
dancing killer
You just a
dancing killer
mid-water-walk
outline all over

the state
I've seen a bullet
become
A cheapskate
Bodies in a
bargain
Handsome but
hardened
Prison era
Spanish cells
Black as well

Run tell about my level
And what you've seen me do to water
And what you've seen me to do men
The last of a dying group of friends
Another city ends.

Day One. Hard Headed

We do a drug of no texture and argue to lose
We laugh in mean times
She dresses in yellow
I pace with the phone
I'm telling her the truth
Her street should have told her about me
but I guess it wanted her for itself

A Time of Night

This simple picture is the voice in the back of the room somewhere near the pillow on her side of the bed. It says that the time of interstates may not be over yet, but going home does not mean he's leaving. She loans me the sky and says, "don't leave it how you found it". She holds us down. I'm reborn all the time. A new man stops nodding off. Let's leave the script on the bathroom floor. Let's get the lighting wrong. I can't wait to write her a real love poem. Based on more than what her friend predicts. But hey. This is window talk. The last poem of the night.

Checkout

The curtains remind alcoholics of church. Alcoholics remind me
the room that there is no revolution outside.
The parking lot coughs travelers up through the late morning with
badlands water on their face.
By noon, this thought finally finishes

> Like upright last words
>
> or
>
> Four months of a slowing solo
>
> or
>
> *You know it's over*
> *When a gangster admits*
> *That he doesn't know*

History is funny when visualized at noon:
A dust cloud of human form / Mostly
arms / Flesh / Smoke / Bored / And nowhere / And nice time / And
nickel genocide

Peaceful oddities like the two years before Europe lands
Or
earth tone weapon handles
or
Pages in a projectile's life
Run the air / Over arms / And nice time / And every bucket genius
I know

Conversations in stone colors   See monuments to circus
Clown debates
Clowns who kill / For nickel / And nowhere / And nice time

See fights on worn down routes between worn thin passengers.
Police who have never done one good thing in their tenure. Not

one good thing in their tenure. Yes, police are teachers who fifth
graders remember more than spelling

See human rights in stone color / Under a noon angle / And nice
time / And noon /And nowhere

All funny to me

Lead teeth to copper glory

A 1980s sky
Over life
That is plenty   and cheap

Blood bubble
Get money
Miss the road already

*A gangster who spent a wretched 40 years outdoors battling landmarks
and flag rope*

The poor man's conscience   Eats scraps and ambulance I.V.s
Free ketchup for the people

Pennies on a hotel table
        Remind me of 1980s martyrs
                    When I'm a few hours
                    From gone

We Charge Genocide Again

–RAYMOND ALLEN–
Folsom Street
        Sleepy genius
Sleepy teacher
        Almost tears
–CARL WARD–
City Hall is Human Noise
                    I will be
                    Stopped and Frisked
–JOHNNIE WARREN–
My cellphone proves / it is a lesser god / For the 100th time

28 Hours

                –TRAYVON MARTIN–
                My girlfriend misses me
                –RAMARLEY GRAHAM–
                Democrats flood the Bronx
                Soundview doesn't care
            Which of these two is half asleep?
                            –STEPHON WATTS–
                            My cousin leaves Chicago
                            Chicago is long gone
                            –DWAYNE BROWN–
                            28 hours
                            –REKIA BOYD–
                            28 hours
                            –SHEREESE FRANCIS–
                            28 hours
                            –UNNAMED–

Low Tide Too

You would dwell on violence too. When there are defensive wounds on the walls in a room where you starve until sun up. Wake up and sit. Head held by four hands. Two of them will never exist.

A creature is in the window. You smirk back. Smack his face. So much solitude in first light. There is height in silence. Wake up on a cliff. Pace on four legs. Two of them will never exist.

Like some say Heaven for starters. Forget a high, you need a con artist. You're stuck with this creature and smoke that's lost in its own conversation. You too would forget to make sense.

Gun powder and inanimate apostles
They will fear no deity before you

You too would walk to the kitchen. Put your tears on the table. Put four legs on this feeling. Maybe doze. Wake singing the ballad of a funeral rose. Put pain in the floor. Stare until the tiles are full of ghosts. Glance left and turn a wall into their host. Glance right and turn a wall into their history.

You too would memoir in fiction
Turn down the hallway and herd wolves
Your shepherd's staff swings at sharks

                                        Why not lie your heart away

Your blood is thinner
Your eviction is soon
Your friend is dead
Your children pretend they're full

Your name dangles on an injunction
Your father is homeless
Your neighborhood plots your death

The state plots your death

Your mother does not trust you
You might die this season

    You're breathing air so thick it's like it is breathing you

You are reading eyes for no reason. Hell's sentiment in every blink. You've seen this legion plenty. Your years are stranded. Your relationships are afraid. You are doing a dead man float on quicksand —brave. Your conscience crawls behind a car for cover. Another friend is dead. And white people are everywhere, casually playing God.

Buckets and Bus Stations

1.
Tennessee bound
And Tennessee was bound to do it
Shark to music
It's a pool room in the car
Cigar break

I told you don't be no more than one woman late again
They killed your best friend for those songs
But I bet they don't get you too

2.
Sea drifter in blue
Pea coat on miracle
Clear night for my love
Walk on the gulf
Like we been doing our whole life
A god's voice cracks
We only talking about water, baby
How many times you gonna write letters to the city?
How many times I gotta leave you at home?
You know guns don't really talk
And gods only talk to themselves

I never knew your father
But one drifter to another
I see you never stood a chance

3.
Tornado pick
Tooth pick for mask
I85's gambler

Passed slaver trader' marble
Pass smoke back and forth
To a fork and back
Rec center's crumbling sign
On the back of his knuckles

The man
The myth
The summer
Dust puddle under dirty eyes
Ten numbers to rest
Messed up the cards
A deck of right eyes

I am
—three devils in a joke about a virgin
—worried that too much heaven is possible
—a fan of anxious comics
—waiting behind tornados for food

Another Bench

No concentration in this courtroom

A bunch of B+ students living out their nightmares

How do I plead with a straight face?

Kicked In The Door

From beyond the vigil's skyline
Serious footwork can be seen
Especially when loose acquaintances look at the candles and flowers
with opera violence on their minds

> Introducing you to the colony
> When the concrete was
> in its prime and not for shuffles

> Two different dates share day-
> light
> Slow walk from the store into a
> flash back

Dust doing most of the talking: *Last stand, brother. Weird wars on the street. See me no more. Who's fixing the drinks tonight? Whoever is must be suicidal.*

> There is a chessboard underneath these tough guys

> From beyond the vigil's jungle there is the easy side of
> autobiography
> > A pretty interesting place to start a war from

Front yards are for having problems with the world

An easy range for the angel of everything under the sun: *That's right, man. I can cut my throat with the sun. Hold your breath on that street if that's what you've always done. Dance floor, you say? I'll tell you what says the eyes of them. They say…*

All dust eventually has to be human

For Me

Door handle in the trash / As a man walks away from his family /
Heavy dream of a shoe / Fog soaked family / Sort of says good bye /
More and more mist / More and more

But Born Alone

A liar wouldn't have lived this long

                    —my humor when fences speak

holding a pair of
rambling dice
that have unique tempers and young souls
that say shut up about our city

a lower land me-and-trash water / and humid sips of sunny sickness
here tidal months crash over a coast up (Jackson, Mississippi)'s
dirty sleeve
why lie
the street's teeth are in pieces   there is reservoir art on the faces
of stragglers   there are ants that lack jazz

sad news from back home coolly read *we'll grow up on your behalf*

stumble back to a car full of last stand the truth is stale
but still liquor
Mission Street would be proud of me
I am a mural man
Almost organized
remember when my lungs would wake up last
walking all morning when it was worth it
watching tired blue
climb over buildings

baby, I'm three decades homeless
and reservoir art is all I ever see
and I'm 2,000 miles from my first fight

maybe no one really survived
maybe I wrote my first poem for no reason

Love, Tongo

Searching for a medicine woman in the strength of my fingers

Really fighting hard
For a retreating grey sky

Remembering nothing

And of all these visitors
It's her that reminds me that I am alone

I can mix a thousand rooms into this anger

I cannot stop here

A Page Tucked Between Candles and Flowers
or
Willie B. Rest When You Feel Like It

And we been knew heaven years ago

                              —a black jacket remarks

heaven becomes our block's shoulders
which are his
which is home grown cadence

        on city bus-rubber and brief eyes—the saint of strays
—San Francisco story

Slight of street
Which is his

Little
brother
slides

Andover smoke says

                    —still

The Love Poems

Mississippi does
have a rush to it
        skydive down Terry Rd.
        black altitude
        to a tuned piano

                two futures watch and wager
                about the strength of a
                Saturday night parking lot in one man
                And his third row family

About how cheap September is. How it might tell the man to *fish
smooth and use those red eyes with all this tall grass and group study.*

Even if we are killed. We have made it out alive, you can hear August
pray. *Bones for souls. Bones for a thousand souls.*

Tall grass pews and gray sky pulpit for anyone in Mississippi
Tinted and rushing
And making
This point

A Downtown Day near Timid Stray Dogs

My back to rusted tanks
On trains traveling through america's night
Ghost downtown howling *Govern yourselves*

25 stories at most
eye level masters
the last world moves
about pothole business
here
america sits decades dead
calming music
rusted track literature
cousin labor
middle class clothes
grenade pin
—grin and posture
pistol and polite
we shake hands forever, I guess
72 hour stranger
I had her at nod

On a one way sidewalk to everywhere
Wait for me
I'm never more than 15 minutes from home

My Personal Deep South

Gray paint and pin drop

Beside me here
Hustling

Weeds and reputation gain image

Antebellum blood and cracked tissue
Gain this stranger

Under consolation trees
And downtown drizzle

A long stare for shelter

Reminds me of
Hannibal's demands
Or the way diamond backs spit
Or smaller pictures
Or the first piece you ever took outside

A million short breaths—if survival

And it's all gray, little brother

Gray and silent

French Quarter Microphone

The lower case French
Got five dollars out of me
Tease thought out of corny trim
And indentured servitude
Incorporated
Near a fire place to nowhere
Great great grandparent marble
Suffering
All this corny shit
Patrons
Are a sight
For suicidal ideation
Don't forget the corny hats
On patrons and servants
Serial gentrifyer's war stories
Corny hats
And trim
And bar tab tall tales
—are the spoils of genocide
don't forget the flight injustices
and lower case French chairs
that mock servants and me
and probably the French
now lower case colonialists
a good friend of mine told me
California hates Black people
Here too

Movie Star

You can tell by my car's wheels that everyone who has ridden with me isn't still alive. Also, that I like my drinks neat, bottled, and in a bus stop... Also, that we are drowning in precinct paper, department store floor plans, and applications to the moon. We can change the color of our snot from gifted to heart attack. I'll tell you about ashes later... But where are all these angels coming from smelling like the cigarette that fails? And why is the man on the safe side of these headlights freezing up?

—If you got nothing to say at my funeral, I'll speak on your behalf.

Snuck Between Pews

The meek church version of the Big City only tells a few stories. Similarly, we will inherit the subway trains. Dutch comedy is uncle to the pollution mortared bricks.

Screams reached black minds. Black minds reached August. August reached the sky
200 years later. Where the last crack of whips go.

"Reverend" is our favorite word this year in the big city. Words we choose from the sacred pollution that only songwriters see.

A bunch of slang about August. Brought down to lay bricks. And the contradictions of faith

Hollywood

California fiction — as experienced the first 20 minutes awake:
A damn steel garden of tubes and countdowns

Hollywood — as experienced the first 20 minutes awake: Let's go
outside and test out looks against the locals

Fight the urge to drop kick their anorexic dogs: Literally

All I remember from the *last time* is the nearest pool table / A
righteous record store / And a prostitute that almost took me to the
movies

Oh and a velvet rope
Made into Uzi rounds

Bring anything
To a L.A. Fight

California Again

A mist of police
through Alleys and Strips

        river
   up
While

imperialism's middle class / doesn't forget to buy
organic / nor / teenage peasants in bulk

White people will never go home
—They will make colonialism work

                Human life with no era
                ecosystems with no expiration
                consumer headache
                stoner headache
      Strip   mall   teeth

Degenerating safety
   Degenerating everything
      Well-manicured suicide and hamburger dates
         August 4th American flags and highway fish

We will all be arrested tomorrow

Garbage Day

He's a marked man if these pennies ever seen one.

Every inanimate object in this room collectively decide to take a
breath in order to demonstrate how fast this man may be gone.

Child soldiers decide to stop breathing in order to demonstrate that
it's never personal.

Grab a stick if you scared   Grab match stick and meet this addiction like
a man
A million fights want to jump down your mind

—Says the pennies. Say the pennies often

Child soldiers coughing at the ground reminds the man who
marked him. Reminds him who to shoot at, and when.

Did they really stop breathing? Did these child soldiers really all
stop breathing at the same time to become inanimate characters
jumping down his mind? How do children become metal in the gas
station?

Metal tumbling out of distracted homes
In a city that has dropped them from its language
Since we going to have no words that mean personal.

We tell him ignore everything in this room except the pennies
Look in the mirror and only see the mark
We say, remember when you were metal

And watch with a grin all the bullshit that jumps down your mind

One of a million faucets around here / drops polluted water into one of a million hands / of one of a million men / *marked men*

Marked man in the mirror before he goes to work and yes just leaving the house is work around here.

The pollution is made of	a white city's dream of flushing
The poor onto the poor	the pollution imagines
All the possibilities	of concentrated surrender

And new shoes stacked to the sky. The garbage sits overflowing in the mouths of politicians. *Waste is the perfect waterfall food.*

Children sort of go to school / they awkwardly run backwards on legs that rotate strangely / when they run sideways you know that a storm is coming / *because sideways you can trust and distrust everyone at the same time*

A parade of television characters dance through the avenues at night. You and I see them when we look out of our windows / but the homeless do not / we know the homeless do not because if they did, *many a bottle would be thrown* ------businesses close with tears instead of chains wrapped around their security doors / we cannot believe that they want sympathy let alone a memorial service------ you and I are perpetually chased by stuffed police through the complex / we lose on purpose / *to show younger brothers and sisters the best way to kill*------the weather industry (*and there is one*) dabbles in housing and decides nobody born from a mother will get a cut— you and I have not eaten for weeks / we try to figure out why / but not for that long / we have tv characters to chase.
.......*Marked man if we ever seen one*.......

New York Because I Said So

A day of minutes,
seconds like leaves. Like leaves are disloyal city characters in brittle
congregations. Near shelter dirt and department store cigarette
breaks.

Stale Irish brew,
peels the white away from midmorning eyes that are already three
lies awake.
And to make matters worse, our hearts are broken.

Next morning,
our story starts more specific. Hearts don't matter here

Tiled grogginess,
tiling grogginess. A slow flying gutter puddle accompanies a man's
cage walk. Defines his punchline altitude.

This building works hard / This building works the same job for
three generations / This building works as long as epochs produce
money and minstrels / One third of this building does not know it
is a third / It woke up groggy / We want to get high

Imagine meaningless water
Imagine orphans making a pact to never have kids
Imagine going to work
—this is our first sip

Who knew that concrete would play such a big part in ecological
facts and that mid morning eyes would leak surprise and hate
laughter. Overcrowded is the emotion of conspiracy and toy
property rights

There's only two kinds of people in this world:
One kind owes you money

Category rooftops / Capitalism stands flamboyant / In lines that
wrap around water fronts / People pass through / Cadillac
swimmers / And children who walk on water / Category
rooftops / That building means margin / Half block toy
shelf / Gladiator industry / The Nothing business / The
nobody / There's a figure in the window / Why does it always look
nervous

> The 5 train has pillow cases
> throughout its Franklin Ave.
> station / Subway station police
> remind me of pillow cases

Soundless playground
—this 3am train—
                Childish economics in full self-portrait
        enthusiasm

In vulnerable slumps,
we race whistling tracks to some cousin of health. This is your city.
Your underground.

> This
> anonymously
> high   floor
> became a friend
> who   doesn't
> know me
> A   writer's
> mountain where
> lineage collapses
> its   span   into

                                        your girlfriend's
                                        cigarette

Also, where strangers lend me temper and proletariat lunch.

Arms between bricks and
midtown fantasy

A manic border
—sort of back then

                        Enemies
             Will not see each other later
                In america's heaven

New York,
Because I said so

It's Midnight Already

Capitalists eat until the world is blurry to them
These streets are made of saliva
Some people are made of saliva too (usually uniformed)

While the crazy man spins around and around (trying to make a
record out of this mass production jungle)

Maybe I'll join him   count cash and cry

                                        These streets are made of saliva
                                And white sheets are worn by a building
                        In which children are supposed to learn how to read well
                                        (white sheets on the highway too)

another mayor puts his head on a pike
(one down is just one down)
but tell all this to the masses and your teacher
will pipeline you

they told me I was jewelry. They told me this was jungle (well
maybe not jungle. More like fifty machine guns planted in the
ground)

it's raining faces again in California
(what does this say about heaven?
What does this say about the people
you have killed?)

                                        waiting lines got so exhausted
                                        that a million minds dropped
                                                all these faces
                                                at the same time

If the fascists can read the lips of a giant that is talking in its sleep, we might as well make our demands in prison letters (today, was born the most important trigger finger in the world). Today, I have begun counting down the pages between now and a pile of books by the tunnel.

Chicago is going to walk out of Chicago one day

Babies will drag street signs like old toys

(today the most important letter left prison)

Babies will laugh at flags like faces who have disappeared. (Maybe I'll join them.) But for now, these streets are made of saliva and we raise half full glasses to the basements that meant nothing and the working poor who lived there. We get shot. We get white sheets on California where the kitchen table likes to talk as much as the walls and romance on the porch consists of hard residing. I mean in this picture, characters talk spit and know that they are hard to kill (the kitchen table knows this too and the porch is almost convinced)

One down is just one down

> This town is coming to town
> A circus watching itself
> Half distracted (half suicidal)

Thrilled children dressed as cops.
(Thrilled children) preaching and policing and intaking and hiring and snatching your money   (This town is coming to town
> with tough trademarks to follow)

Today I watched capitalism walk on water. And people play dead.
So that they could be part of a miracle

Near 6th Street

Alley dweller mime moves within
A perpetual middle
In an alley of landfill manners
And the first world's peculiar beds
Mime asks a child *What do you see?*
Child replies *Hands being hands in a landfill*
And I see that the rich hate us
Now the child may go

Mime moves on
Becomes the bones for death row shapes
More peculiar beds
Cargo in courts
Now the needle may go

Innocent ghosts interested in this alley
Decide to stay
We have run out of middle
And now you may go

Internationalism

This night feels the same to *Tall Baby*. As he watches winos who are *dressed as rattlesnakes*. All in a *cocky holocaust* that is too young to dress down. Around here, citizens eat the chaser and *prove that they got revenge* by their storecounter rapport. There are new loads of *baby teeth shipped daily*. The working class is in heaven, over / but ignoring miles and miles of their work. This every kind of yard knows. This night feels the same. Rattlesnakes near spit and wine. *Tall Baby fishes for lighter and sees no leaders*. Sees a mother, the first Sabbath after losing her son, walk and wheeze. Everywhere is blades. With soundless imagination, streets die then smile. *Tall Baby* nods once. Thinks of heaven. A look to the left will have to do. Because you *never look up when you're near spit and wine*, and the rich man's eager. *Tall Baby* thinks, same shit / different decorations. *Tall Baby shoots back*. The skyline has gone sideways. *Rooftops have become gun barrels*. There will never be cover again. Millions surrender. *Tall Baby's* walls only want to talk about the topic of *hinges in times of holocaust*. On a free trade Sabbath, skyline returns to its feet. On a free trade Sabbath, skyline marches. Puts boot to fracture—babies in heaven. *The real heaven*. Over red and shanty. *Ignoring nothing*. This every kind of yard knows. On a free trade Sabbath, skyline returns to first world. Somewhere in a shipping company state, *Tall Baby* talks to gates. He's been faceless for months. A self-taught city says only whites are welcome. *That city is a proud bastard still*, when *Tall Baby* returns.

It's Winter Already

and if the murder rate wasn't enough, babies stopped crying on my street.
Now every last one us for twenty stop signs have no ambition.

> *Maybe I should take it*
> *One store front at a time*
> *Like that woman pushing*
> *A shopping cart full of*
> *First world magic dust*
> *Talking to me about*

Splitting seconds, son, into
As many back alleys
As our minds want to see no farther than the limits
Of this city, understand?

I developed a thing for assembly lines back when I was ten and cops started
running my name. when a break-through riot would have been nice.

> *And I am still worthy of*
> *the nickname a heroin addict gave me*
> *And I'm still supposed to let him take it back in a matter of daybreak.*

I think I will take this show to the graveyard. One store front at a time
can mean anything, the dead will probably say. Then turn around before I
finish agreeing.

I'm late checking in, son, and the assembly line is spitting on me
and you. *We will have no more of this city.*

She says,
Somewhere in the shock of a four wall winter, son, I decided to go
wherever I wanted to go.
San Francisco got me up its sleeve. Got me on all roads. Got
ghosts minding my tires.

> Fight the world with me. Where broken dishes
> become pieces of children. We were sad too. San

Francisco never been about its skyline. It's broken dishes
and lit cigarettes on the back of the bus. It's the trickster.
A bored trickster. Snorting Victorians with people still in
them. I was the queen of the movie
I was the crowd favorite
I was lost in the wooden thoughts of a piano raised scholar
I was the first hustler ever born

For the 14 Mission St.

In his pockets it is winter already
knuckle—then wrist   psalm
in street green letters
here lies   in half asleep young skin   a tattered page one

page one:
all stair cases are open air
and will be the first to talk
if the poor so wills it

page two:
pieces of subtitles
mouths talk last

—in his pockets
it is midnight already—

page three:
someone's dead already
someone has taught him psalm

page four:
every system is suicidal
the poor so will it

bus loops its route
last stop
already

let him sleep again

stair / case / air

California vs Kid

Eye to eye with the lowest branch

Crying breath into the hands of an avenue

Shirt made somewhere in the land of first hand

Shoes witness an informal prayer

Trash wasn't yet trash
Talk wasn't yet mine
Running away never really was running away

I know you see me
What should I call you?
I will never be anything that you need to forgive

Mali

I am the son of a hospital room
In a world of bed pans
Water does not know its own

I strain to hear every narrator in the room
They are the cycling shifts in his face
A side-less supernatural
His faces
That strain and strain
Collapse and shoot
Freeze then fade
Wander in then wander away
Let's live this hour with no meaning

I am a son   He is a finish
I think this been more for you than for me, I say

And we smile
          like water would

What I know now. There was a dark red Sunday sitting under that
Wednesday afternoon. A dark red Sunday. A wolf wearing mild
skies. What I know now. Chicago Streets. Collect and guard Souls.
Sons respect their last breath fathers. Fathers pass away in between
two conversations. I know that our blood is one thousand bullets
here. We. Are. Skin. And. Edge. Fast hands. Hunched rivers.
Prison Canvas. Strange leaves. We agree.
                         Are organized
                         Now named

More prison.
More canvas.

More generals reach womb.
More sketches reach son
—I should talk to his ghost with a prison pencil

Grew up watching sketched women and men
turn then walk away from the foreground.
Cardboard can look that deep.
43rd Street Collected Souls.

Pops,
As you travel where light means
a little less and home perhaps more

Be any man that suits you
Shift low air
Kneel in hurricane
Splash a bending image over your face
Perhaps an image of us
Walk east, I guess

Eat hurricane
Let this lonely love you
Do not sing
Do not understand
Do nothing for now
Do not belong

Perhaps, see us again

The Dedication

Quilt of oaths

When I get there
Let her be my first teacher

Tell me the story
That set my grandfather free

Pick the first few notes
And I'll play the new middle

Pick something to smile about
And I'll lay my face down
With gun handles
And guitar picks

Walk groundless

Easy even

Born in San Francisco, Tongo Eisen-Martin is a movement worker, educator, and poet who has organized against mass incarceration and extra-judicial killing of Black people throughout the United States. He has educated in detention centers from New York's Rikers Island to California's San Quentin State Prison. His work in Rikers Island was featured in the New York Times. He was also adjunct faculty at the Institute for Research in African-American Studies at Columbia University in New York. Subscribing to the Freirian model of education, he designed curricula for oppressed people's education projects from San Francisco to South Africa. His latest curriculum on extra-judicial killing of Black people, *We Charge Genocide Again*, has been used as an educational and organizing tool throughout the country. He uses his craft to create liberated territory wherever he performs and teaches. He recently lived and organized around issues of human rights and self-determination in Jackson, MS.

CPSIA information can be obtained
at www.ICGtesting.com
Printed in the USA
LVHW090441210322
713941LV00002B/136

9 780988 610835